A Bill's Journey into Law

by Suzanne Slade

illustrated by Tony Trimmer

HR - 1000

PICTURE WINDOW BOOKS

a capstone imprint

Special thanks to our advisers for their expertise:
Betsy Sinclair, PhD, Assistant Professor of Political Science
University of Chicago

Terry Flaherty, PhD, Professor of English
Minnesota State University, Mankato

Editor: Jill Kalz
Designer: Tracy Davies
Art Director: Nathan Gassman
Production Specialist: Sarah Bennett
The illustrations in this book were created with mixed media/found object.

Picture Window Books
1710 Roe Crest Drive
North Mankato, MN 56003
www.capstonepub.com

All books published by Picture Window Books are manufactured
with paper containing at least 10 percent post-consumer waste.

Library of Congress Cataloging-in-Publication Data
Slade, Suzanne.
  A bill's journey into law / by Suzanne Slade ; illustrated by Tony
Trimmer.
      p. cm. — (Follow It!)
  Includes index.
  ISBN 978-1-4048-6831-1 (library binding)
  ISBN 978-1-4048-7027-7 (paperback)
  1. Bill drafting—United States—Juvenile literature. 2.
Legislation—United States—Juvenile literature. 3. Legislative
bodies—United States—Juvenile literature. I. Trimmer, Tony. II.
Title.
  KF4950.S53 2012
  328.73'077—dc22   2011006500

Printed in the United States of America in North Mankato, Minnesota.
062018
000672

Today is Ramesh's favorite day of the year—his birthday.

Ramesh loves presents and cake. But he loves eating ice cream most of all. As he blows out the candles, Ramesh makes a special wish.

3

Ramesh thinks free ice cream would make lots of people happy. He wonders if his idea could become a law. He calls the congressperson who represents his state to find out.

The U.S. Congress makes laws for the country. Congress is run by two groups, the House of Representatives and the Senate. If a representative or senator agrees to sponsor an idea, it may be introduced as a bill. Then it has a chance of becoming a law.

The congressperson takes Ramesh's idea to the
Capitol Building in Washington, D.C.

She types up the idea and turns it into a bill. The bill gets its own number.

The congressperson drops the bill into a wooden box called a hopper. Now the bill is ready to be introduced to Congress.

From idea to paper in no time flat!

HR - 1000

Thousands of new bills are introduced into Congress every year. Only about 4 percent become laws.

The bill is sent to a committee of the House of Representatives. Committee members talk about the new bill.

How many scoops of free ice cream would each person get?

One scoop for each year?

I love being the center of attention.

HR - 1000

The House of Representatives has many committees that study new bills. Each committee specializes in certain areas, such as education or agriculture (farming). The Senate has its own committees that look at new bills.

Now the bill is put on the House of Representatives' calendar. There it waits and waits.

When the bill's big day comes, some representatives find problems with the bill. Others try to solve them.

Some people can't eat food made from milk. They're lactose intolerant.

They could have sorbet or sherbet, instead. No milk in those.

Boy, these people can talk.

HR-1000

After the group shares its ideas, the representatives vote. More than half vote yes, so the bill continues its journey.

The U.S. House of Representatives has 435 members. A bill needs more than half of the representatives to vote for it in order to pass.

HR-1000

The bill moves on to a Senate committee. Members look over the bill carefully. They ask more questions.

What if someone says it's his birthday every month?

Should people have to prove their birthday somehow?

How about birth certificates?

The committee members stay up late talking about the bill.

Anyone else getting sleepy?

When it's time for a vote, the bill passes. It's off to the Senate!

The senators think of questions no one has asked yet: How will we pay for all this free ice cream? Taxes? What about people who don't have an ice-cream shop nearby? Can someone get a rain check if she's sick on her birthday?

After many days, each senator votes. There are more "yeas" than "nays," so the bill keeps moving.

There are 100 senators in the U.S. Senate. Two are elected from each state. Like in the House, a majority must vote in favor of a bill for it to pass. In the Senate, "yea" means yes, and "nay" means no.

After passing the House and the Senate, the bill is printed on official paper. Two important people, the vice president of the United States and the Speaker of the House, sign the bill.

But the journey's not over yet! Next stop? The White House.

I'm so nervous. I'm going to meet the president!

A bill may have many changes, or amendments, during its journey to become a law. Both the House and the Senate must give the amendments the OK.

In his oval office, the president reads every word of the bill. He thinks about lots of things. Will this bill help people? Is it fair? How much will it cost?

If the president does not like a bill, he or she can veto it. A vetoed bill may still become law if two-thirds of the members in both the House of Representatives and Senate pass the bill again.

The president smiles and grabs a new pen.
He signs the bill and makes it a law.

Now Ramesh, and everyone else in the United States, will enjoy free birthday ice cream!

Diagram of a Bill's Journey

Idea

Sponsored by congressperson

Bill

Discussed and voted on by the House Committee

Discussed and voted on by the House of Representatives

Discussed and voted on by the Senate Committee

Discussed and voted on by the Senate

Vice president, Speaker of the House, and president sign the bill

LAW

(Note: If the bill does not pass one of the voting sessions at any point, it "dies." It does not continue its journey.)